Picture the Past
LEISURE

Jane Shuter

Heinemann
LIBRARY

First published in Great Britain by Heinemann Library
Halley Court, Jordan Hill, Oxford OX2 8EJ
a division of Reed Educational & Professional Publishing Ltd

OXFORD FLORENCE PRAGUE MADRID ATHENS
MELBOURNE AUCKLAND KUALA LUMPUR SINGAPORE TOKYO
IBADAN NAIROBI KAMPALA JOHANNESBURG GABORONE
PORTSMOUTH NH (USA) CHICAGO MEXICO CITY SAO PAULO

Designed by Ken Vail Graphic Design, Cambridge
Colour separations by Dot Gradations, Wickford, Essex
Printed in Malaysia by Times Offset (M) Sdn. Bhd.

01 00 99 98
10 9 8 7 6 5 4 3 2 1

ISBN 0 431 04267 5

British Library Cataloguing in Publication Data

Shuter, Jane
  Leisure – (Picture the past)
  1. Amusements – History – Juvenile literature
  2. Amusements – Pictorial works – Juvenile literature
  I. Title
  790'.09

This book is also available in a hardback library edition, ISBN 0 431 04266 7

Acknowledgements
The authors and publishers would like to thank the following for permission to use
photographs and other illustrative material:
Beck Isle Museum, page 4 top;
Curtis Museum, Alton, page 6;
The Peter Gillies Collection, page 4 bottom;
Newport County Records Office, page 8;
Oxfordshire Photographic Archive, page 10;
Popperfoto, pages 12, 16;
Topham Picturepoint, pages 5, 14, 18, 20.

Cover photographs reproduced with permission of Oxfordshire Photographic
Archive, Newport County Records Office and Popperfoto.

Our thanks to Betty Root for her comments in the preparation of this book.

Every effort has been made to contact copyright holders of any material reproduced
in this book. Any omissions will be rectified in subsequent printings if notice is
given to the Publisher.

Contents

Some words are shown in bold text, **like this**. You can find out what these words mean by looking in the glossary on page 24.

Taking photos

People started taking photos in the 1830s. It took over an hour to take a photo! By the 1860s it only took 15 minutes.

When cameras were first invented, they could only take black and white photos. If people wanted colour photos they had to paint them by hand.

This photo of a family watching TV was taken in the 1950s, when TV was a new invention. TV screens were very small and the picture was black and white, not colour.

Playing croquet, 1865

In this photo the Curtis family are playing **croquet** in their garden. People with big gardens often played croquet.

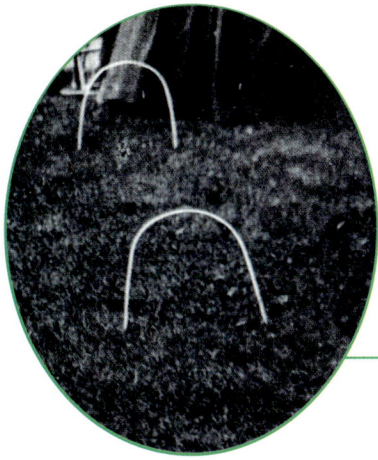

In croquet, each person has a ball which they have to hit through all the **hoops**.

They hit the ball with a heavy stick. It is called a **mallet**.

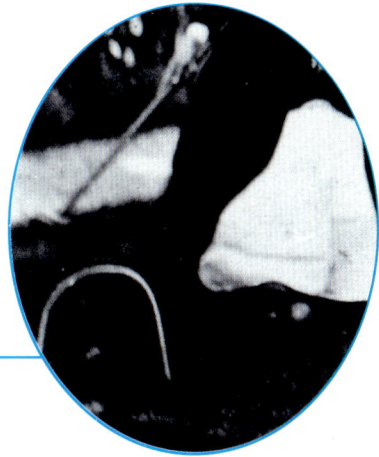

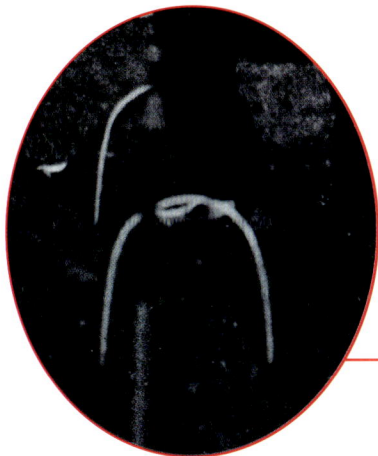

They have to get the ball to this post at the end.

Can you find

- a woman with an umbrella to keep off the sun?
- four croquet balls?
- how many hats are there?

Ventnor, Isle of Wight, 1890

People believed that the seaside was good for you, as well as fun. Queen Victoria's doctor said Ventnor was a very healthy place to visit.

People rented a **bathing machine** to change into their swimsuits.

Swimming costumes covered up much of the body.

This woman has an umbrella to keep the sun off her.

Can you find

- the 'Gentlemen's Bathing Office', where men rent bathing machines?
- two boys playing a ball game?
- five umbrellas?

The fair, Oxford, 1901

The fair in this photo is full of people having fun. There is still a fair in Oxford every year.

At fairs there were lots of **shows** for people to watch.

The show started when someone banged the drum outside.

The pictures outside told people what they would see in the show.

Can you find
- the drums for the dog and monkey show?
- a picture of a dog balancing on a ball?
- some monkeys tied to a rail?

Picking hops, 1901

Not many people could pay to go away on holiday at this time. Some people worked in the country as a holiday. These people are in Kent, picking **hops**.

Poor people went hop picking. But richer people did too.

The hop plants climb up the poles. They twist round and round.

The pickers can't reach the tops of the poles! They cut the hops down with a tool.

Can you find

- the box for the picked hops?
- where the hop boxes will go? (Read the label!)
- six different sorts of hat?

A football match, 1925

In this photo, big crowds have come to watch Sheffield United play football with Cardiff City. It is an important match – the Cup Final at Wembley.

The policemen are watching the match too!

The crowd is almost all men. There are no adverts around the pitch.

The man in ordinary clothes on the pitch is not from the crowd. He is the referee.

Can you find

- the policemen in the crowd?
- the person photographing the match?
- the ballboy, watching to see if the ball goes out?

Listening to the radio, 1940

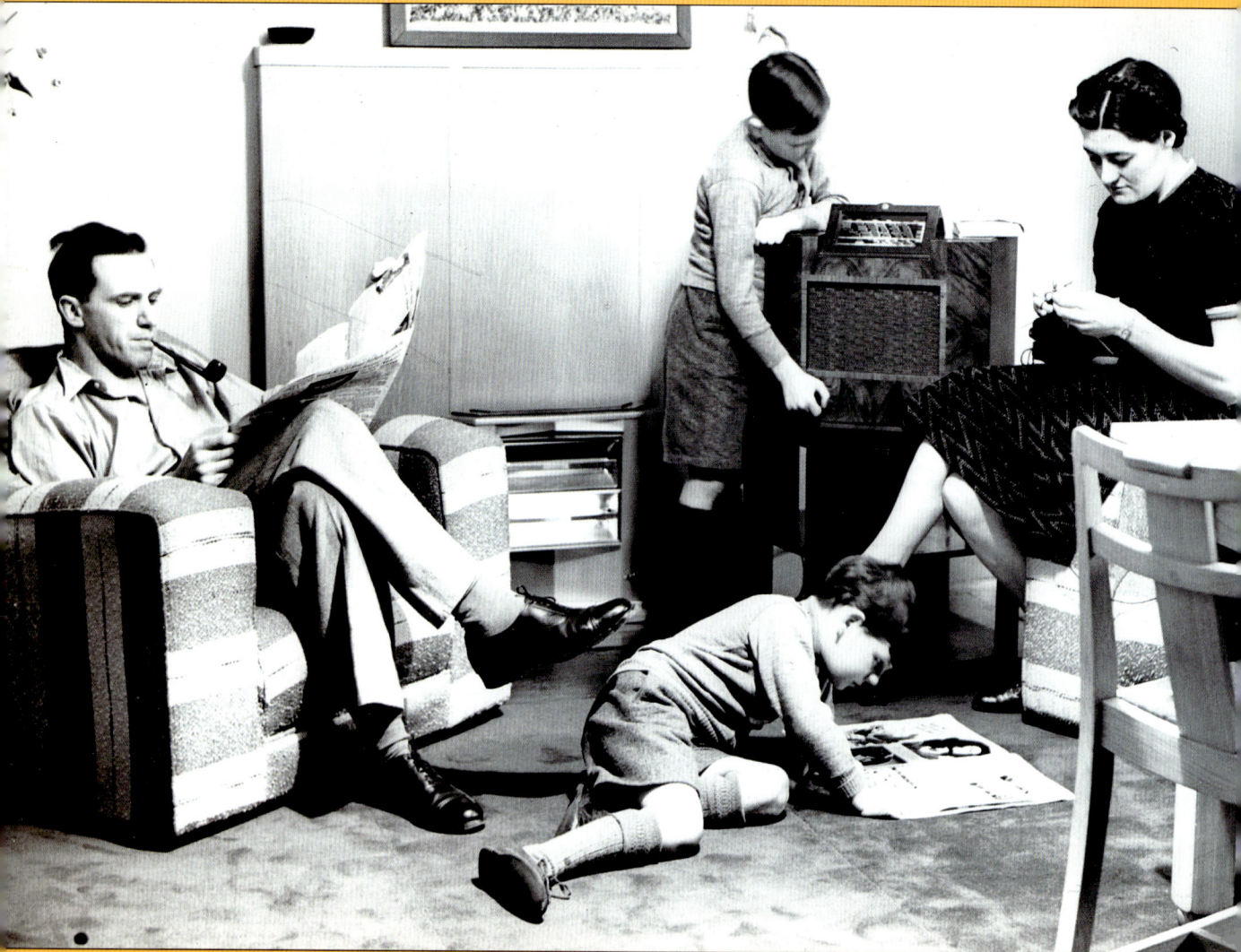

The family in this photo are listening to the news on the radio. TVs had been invented, but they cost a lot of money. Hardly anyone had a TV.

This was used to 'tune in' (find the right programme).

The sound came out of a speaker in here.

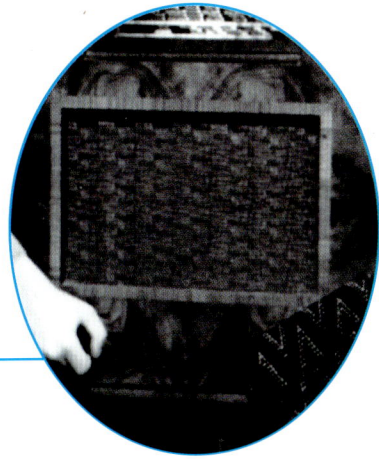

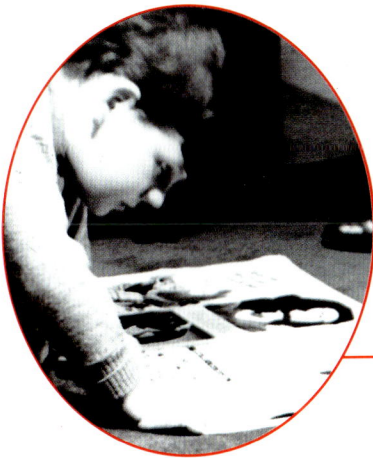

People did things while they listened to the radio. One boy is reading.

Can you find
- what Dad is doing?
- what Mum is doing?
- the switch to turn the electric fire on?

Cinema queue, 1947

The people in this photo are queuing for the cinema. There is a queue each side of the cinema. Some people will have to wait a long time to get in.

'Gone with the Wind' is a very long film. People took sandwiches with them!

The small cinema next door shows news films. Most people could only see films of things that were in the news by going to the cinema.

Can you find
- the name of the cinema?
- the lion's head on the front of the cinema?
- a clock?

Littlehampton beach, 1952

This photo was taken in June. Lots of people are on their holidays. Very few people went abroad for a holiday at that time.

Buckets and spades were made of metal, painted with bright colours.

This boy is having fun squirting someone!

Some people kept their clothes on to sit in the sun.

What's different?

Look at the photo on page 8. What's different in 1952? Think about:

- what people are wearing
- what they are doing on the beach.

Did you find?

Playing croquet, 1865, pages 6–7
- five hats

Ventnor, Isle of Wight, 1890, pages 8–9

The fair, Oxford, 1901, pages 10–11

Picking hops, 1901,
pages 12–13

A football match, 1925,
pages 14–15

Listening to the
radio, 1940,
pages 16–17

Cinema queue, 1947,
pages 18–19

Glossary (What words mean)

bathing machine a small shed on wheels where people changed out of ordinary clothes into swimming things. Some bathing machines were pulled into the water by horses, so people could get into the water without being seen.

croquet a game where people have to knock a ball through lots of hoops to reach a post stuck in the ground

hoop a curved piece of wire which has both ends sticking in the ground

hops special flowers of the hop plant that are used to make beer

mallet a wooden stick that is used for hitting things

show something people pay to go and see. It can be a collection of things, or an act put on by animals or people.

Index